STEPHEN CURRY

KENNY ABDO

Bolt!

An Imprint of Abdo Zoom
abdopublishing.com

abdopublishing.com

Published by Abdo Zoom, a division of ABDO, P.O. Box 398166, Minneapolis,
Minnesota 55439. Copyright © 2019 by Abdo Consulting Group, Inc. International
copyrights reserved in all countries. No part of this book may be reproduced in any
form without written permission from the publisher. Bolt!™ is a trademark and logo
of Abdo Zoom.

Printed in the United States of America, North Mankato, Minnesota.
052018
092018

Photo Credits: Alamy, AP Images, Icon Sportswire, iStock
Production Contributors: Kenny Abdo, Jennie Forsberg, Grace Hansen
Design Contributors: Dorothy Toth, Neil Klinepier

Library of Congress Control Number: 2017960655

Publisher's Cataloging-in-Publication Data

Names: Abdo, Kenny, author.
Title: Stephen Curry / by Kenny Abdo.
Description: Minneapolis, Minnesota : Abdo Zoom, 2019. | Series: Sports biographies |
    Includes online resources and index.
Identifiers: ISBN 9781532124815 (lib.bdg.) | ISBN 9781532124952 (ebook) |
    ISBN 9781532125027 (Read-to-me ebook)
Subjects: LCSH: Curry, Stephen, 1988-, Biography--Juvenile literature. |
    Guards (Basketball)--Biography-- Juvenile literature. | Basketball players--
    United States--Biography--Juvenile literature. | Golden State Warriors
    (Basketball team)--Biography--Juvenile literature.
Classification: DDC 796.323092 [B]--dc23

TABLE OF CONTENTS

Stephen Curry 4

Early Years. 8

Going Pro. 12

Legacy 20

Glossary 22

Online Resources 23

Index 24

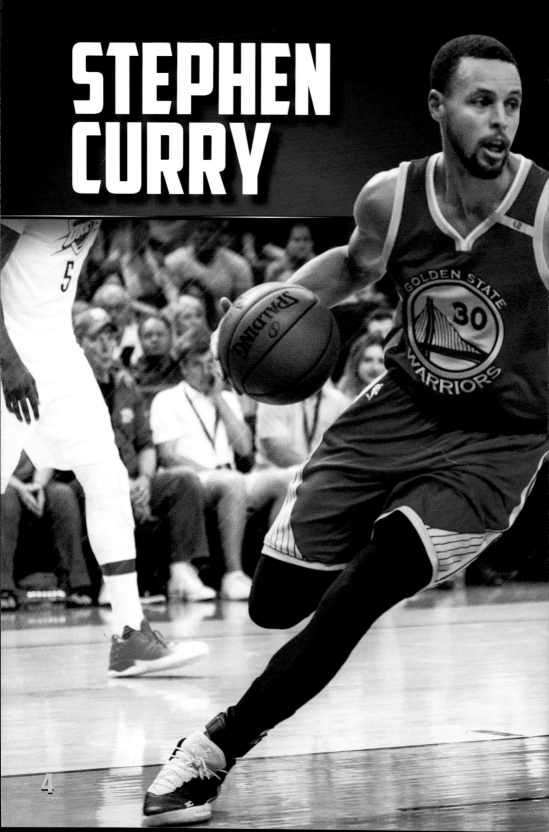

STEPHEN CURRY

At just 6ft 3in (1.9m), Stephen
Curry is short for an NBA player.
But that does not stop him from
being a stellar point guard for the
Golden State Warriors.

He is known as the first player in NBA history to be elected Most Valuable Player (MVP) by a **unanimous** vote. He is also considered the greatest shooter in the game.

EARLY YEARS

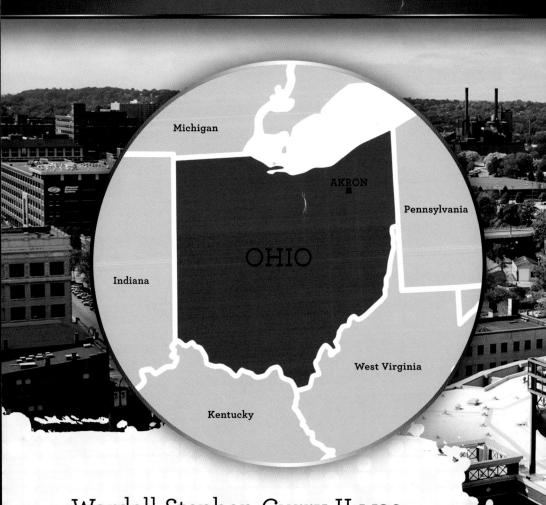

Wardell Stephen Curry II was born in Akron, Ohio, in 1988.

His father was also a professional basketball player. Curry learned the **basics** of basketball by practicing with him.

In high school, Curry was named all-conference, all-state, and led his team to three state **playoffs**. He got national attention for his skills at Davidson College.

GOING PRO

Curry was **drafted** by the Golden State Warriors in 2009.

R. RUBIO 10 BUCKS

15 PISTONS

VARRIORS GOLDEN STATE WARRIORS

DEN STATE WARRIOR:

GOLDEN STATE WARRIORS GOLDEN STATE V

NBA DRAFT NY 09
PRESENTED BY EA

NBA

As a point guard, he got more than 22 points per game. Curry was put on the NBA All-Rookie First Team in 2010. In 2011, he won the Skills Challenge at the NBA All-Star Weekend.

Curry sprained his ankle many times through his first few seasons. In 2011, he had surgery to fix his ankle and got back on the court.

In 2014, Curry and Klay Thompson formed the "Splash Brothers." They led the Warriors in a 16-game winning **streak**.

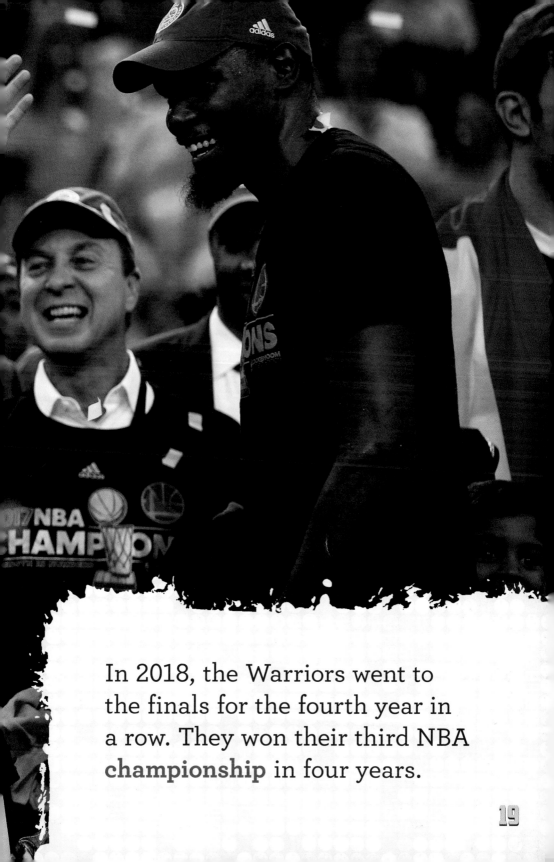

In 2018, the Warriors went to the finals for the fourth year in a row. They won their third NBA **championship** in four years.

LEGACY

Curry is one of only 11 players to win the MVP award two years in a row.

Curry **volunteers** regularly for charity. He raises resources for schools through the Stephen Curry Foundation. He also hosts a pair of charity golf events every year.

GLOSSARY

basics – the starting point to a certain subject or activity.

championship – a game held to find a first-place winner.

draft – a process in sports to assign athletes to a certain team.

playoffs – a best of seven tournament to determine who the best basketball team is.

streak – a period of continual wins.

unanimous – when everyone fully agrees on something.

volunteer – to offer to give one's time to help others without being paid.

ONLINE RESOURCES

Booklinks
NONFICTION NETWORK
FREE! ONLINE NONFICTION RESOURCES

To learn more about Stephen Curry, please visit **abdobooklinks.com**. These links are routinely monitored and updated to provide the most current information available.

INDEX

awards 7, 11, 20

charity 21

Davidson College 11

family 9

Golden State Warriors 5, 12, 17, 19

high school 11

injury 16

MVP 7, 20

NBA Championship 19

Ohio 8

size 5

Thompson, Klay 17